Keep this pocket-sized Frith book with you when you are visiting Berkshire, or if you are on holiday in the locality.

Whether you are in your car or on foot, you will enjoy an evocative journey back in time. Compare the Berkshire of old with what you can see today— see how the towns and villages have changed down the years, how shops and buildings have been replaced; look at fine details such as lamp-posts, shop fascias and trade signs; and see the many alterations to the Berkshire landscape that have taken place unnoticed during our lives, some of which we may have taken for granted.

At the turn of a page you will gain fascinating insights into Berkshire's unique history.

GW00631140

FRANCIS FRITH'S
pocket ALBUM

BERKSHIRE

A POCKET ALBUM

Adapted from an original book by
NICK CHANNER

First published in the United Kingdom in 2005 by
Frith Book Company Ltd

ISBN 1-85937-955-9
Text and Design copyright © Frith Book Company Ltd
Photographs copyright © The Francis Frith Collection

British Library Cataloguing in Publication Data

Berkshire—A Pocket Album
Adapted from an original book by Nick Channer

Frith Book Company Ltd
Frith's Barn, Teffont,
Salisbury, Wiltshire SP3 5QP
Tel: +44 (0) 1722 716 376
Email: info@francisfrith.co.uk
www.francisfrith.co.uk

Printed and bound in Great Britain by MPG, Bodmin

Front Cover: **WARGRAVE, THE VILLAGE** 1890 27177

The colour-tinting is for illustrative purposes only, and is not intended to be historically accurate.

Frontispiece: **MAIDENHEAD, HIGH STREET** 1890 23634

BRAY, LANDING PLACE 1890 23261

CONTENTS

FRANCIS FRITH
VICTORIAN PIONEER

Francis Frith, founder of the world-famous photographic archive, was a complex and multi-talented man. A devout Quaker and a highly successful Victorian businessman, he was philosophic by nature and pioneering in outlook. By 1855 he had already established a wholesale grocery business in Liverpool, and sold it for the astonishing sum of £200,000, which is the equivalent today of over £15,000,000. Now in his thirties, and captivated by the new science of photography, Frith set out on a series of pioneering journeys up the Nile and to the Near East.

INTRIGUE AND EXPLORATION

He was the first photographer to venture beyond the sixth cataract of the Nile. Africa was still the mysterious 'Dark Continent', and Stanley and Livingstone's historic meeting was a decade into the future. The conditions for picture taking confound belief. He laboured for hours in his wicker dark-room in the sweltering heat of the desert, while the volatile chemicals fizzed dangerously in their trays. Back in London he exhibited his photographs and was 'rapturously cheered' by members of the Royal Society. His reputation as a photographer was made overnight.

VENTURE OF A LIFE-TIME

By the 1870s the railways had threaded their way across the country, and Bank Holidays and half-day Saturdays had been made obligatory by Act of Parliament. All of a sudden the working man and his family were able to enjoy days out, take holidays, and see a little more of the world.

With typical business acumen, Francis Frith foresaw that these new tourists would enjoy having souvenirs to commemorate their days out. For the next thirty years he travelled the country by train and by pony and trap, producing fine photographs of seaside resorts and beauty spots that were keenly bought by millions of Victorians. These prints were painstakingly pasted into family albums and pored over during the dark nights of winter, rekindling precious memories of summer excursions. Frith's studio was soon supplying retail shops all over the country, and by 1890 F Frith & Co had become the greatest specialist photographic publishing company in the world, with over 2,000 sales outlets, and pioneered the picture postcard.

FRANCIS FRITH'S LEGACY

Francis Frith had died in 1898 at his villa in Cannes, his great project still growing. The archive he created continued in business for another seventy years. By 1970 it contained over a third of a million pictures showing 7,000 British towns and villages.

Frith's legacy to us today is of immense significance and value, for the magnificent archive of evocative photographs he created provides a unique record of change in the cities, towns and villages throughout Britain over a century and more. Frith and his fellow studio photographers revisited locations many times down the years to update their views, compiling for us an enthralling and colourful pageant of British life and character.

We are fortunate that Frith was dedicated to recording the minutiae of everyday life. For it is this sheer wealth of visual data, the painstaking chronicle of changes in dress, transport, street layouts, buildings, housing, engineering and landscape that captivates us so much today, offering us a powerful link with the past and with the lives of our ancestors.

Computers have now made it possible for Frith's many thousands of images to be accessed almost instantly. The archive offers every one of us an opportunity to examine the places where we and our families have lived and worked down the years. Its images, depicting our shared past, are now bringing pleasure and enlightenment to millions around the world a century and more after his death.

The railway at Datchet runs between the Thames and the village centre. Datchet is mentioned in Shakespeare's 'The Merry Wives of Windsor' and Jerome K Jerome's 'Three Men in a Boat'.

DATCHET

The Green, with its period buildings, lies at the heart of Datchet. This photograph captures an ice cream vendor waiting for business in the village centre. Before the M4 motorway existed, traffic from London came through Datchet en route to Windsor.

DATCHET

THE GREEN AND THE MANOR HOTEL 1950 / D9034

DATCHET
THE VILLAGE 1905 53194

Just before the turn of the century, Datchet suffered serious flooding when the swollen Thames caused a pond in the centre of the village to overflow. Several anxious residents were isolated in their homes.

With their top hats and stiff collars, Eton scholars have been an integral part of daily life in Eton since the College was founded by Henry VI in 1440.

ETON

HIGH STREET 1906 / 56036A

ETON

THE COLLEGE CHAPEL FROM BARNES POOL

BRIDGE 1914 / 67007

The roof of Eton College Chapel, visible in this photograph, is a familiar sight in Eton. With the exception of the chapel, all the college buildings are built of brick — nearly two and a half million of them.

13

This photograph captures the bustle and activity of one of Eton's most colourful events. On 4 June every year a procession of boats takes place to celebrate the birthday of George III, Eton's favourite monarch.

ETON

THE 4TH OF JUNE PROCESSION OF BOATS 1906 / 53724

HOLYPORT

MAIN ROAD 1909 / 61983

Several years after this photograph was taken, the east Berkshire village of Holyport became the setting for a First World War PoW camp and German soldiers were regularly seen marching through the village on daily exercise.

This photograph shows the spire of St Andrew's church at Clewer, which is situated on the Thames, looking up towards Windsor Castle. Many servants of the royal household are buried in its churchyard.

WINDSOR

CLEWER 1890 / 25618

WINDSOR

THE BRIDGE 1895 / 35370

Overlooked by Windsor Castle's famous Round Tower, Windsor Bridge was erected in 1822. Until the 20th century, there was a toll – the living paid 2d, while the departed could be carried across by coffin for 6/8d!

St George's Chapel is the resting place of kings – Henry VIII and Charles I are buried here. The chapel, one of England's most impressive ecclesiastical buildings, was begun by Edward IV in 1475 and completed during the reign of Henry VIII.

WINDSOR

ST GEORGE'S CHAPEL 1895 / 35387

This fascinating photograph shows the intricate detail and sumptuous carving of St George's Chapel. St George's is also the Garter Chapel: above the oak stalls of the knights hang their banners, which remain there until death.

WINDSOR

ST GEORGE'S CHAPEL, CASTLE STREET, WINDSOR
1895 / 35394

WINDSOR

RIVERSIDE GARDENS   1906 / 53721

During the Victorian and Edwardian eras, the Thames riverbank drew large numbers of visitors who came here to enjoy the tranquil scene. Windsor's royal status made this stretch of the river especially popular.

21

This is Windsor Castle's world-famous entrance. By the 16th century, the main gateway was in such a poor state of repair that Henry VIII replaced it with the one that bears his name.

WINDSOR

HENRY VIII GATE 1914 / 66985

WINDSOR

PEASCOD STREET 1937 / 88141

Peascod Street lies at the centre of Windsor, at the top of the hill. The town centre is characterised by its streets of essentially Victorian and Georgian buildings.

WINDSOR

ROMNEY LOCK 1906 / 53722

The village was formerly known as Wyrardisbury, and in medieval times was part of the Crown Lands of Windsor. Magna Carta Island, where the famous charter was signed in 1215, is nearby.

WRAYSBURY
THE FERRY 1890 / 27246

After the death of his mother Queen Victoria, Edward VII did much to promote
Ascot as a significant social event. This photograph of the racecourse was taken a
year after Edward became King.

ASCOT

THE GRANDSTAND 1901 / 46866

Queen Anne established the famous racecourse in 1711, though the meetings only became popular when the Duke of Cumberland, the first member of the Royal Family elected to the Jockey Club, revived them later in the 18th century.

Ascot, close to the Surrey border and situated in a wooded corner of the county that was once part of the ancient Windsor Forest, has a strong suburban feel to it, with an abundance of Edwardian villas and shop fronts.

ASCOT

HIGH STREET 1906 / 55013

When this photograph was taken, Binfield was no more than a sleepy village. The Stag Inn dates back to the 18th century, and the elm tree on the right reputedly marked the centre of Windsor Forest.

BINFIELD

THE STAG 1892 / B97001

More than 50 years before this photograph was taken, Bracknell was described in the county directory as 'a small village consisting of a long, narrow street, inhabited principally by small shopkeepers, who supply the surrounding neighbourhood.'

BRACKNELL

HIGH STREET 1901 / 46893

This photograph shows the shingled spire of Holy Trinity Church peeping above the rooftops in Church Road. Old Bracknell consisted of little more than a few houses and shops before New Town status allowed it to expand virtually beyond recognition.

BRACKNELL

CHURCH ROAD 1901 / 46897

*With New Town status and under the aegis of the
Development Corporation, Bracknell began to expand
rapidly. The town's first factory was in production by 1952;
by the time this photograph was taken, the population had
quadrupled.*

BRACKNELL

HIGH STREET 1961 / B172059

Some time during the second half of the 19th century, Bracknell became a town, helped by the coming of the railway in 1856 and the development of market gardening and brick-making.

BRACKNELL

HIGH STREET 1901 / 46894

Bracknell was not considered the most prosperous of towns before the coming of the railway. Today, it is one of the largest industrial areas in the county.

BRACKNELL

HIGH STREET 1901 / 46895

CROWTHORNE

HIGH STREET 1921 / 69934

The village of Crowthorne takes its name from a group of thorn trees at nearby Brookers Corner. At one time the name 'Albertonville' was suggested in honour of the Prince Consort.

Crowthorne grew and developed mainly as a result of two famous institutions – Wellington College and Broadmoor Hospital – both of which were built in the mid 19th century.

CROWTHORNE

HIGH STREET 1925 / 78030

Crowthorne has expanded in every direction since this photograph was taken. However, the influence of the Roman occupation is still much in evidence. The Devil's Highway, a Roman road, passes through the village, and two Roman milestones can still be seen locally.

CROWTHORNE

1906 / 57016

By the time this photograph was taken, Crowthorne was firmly established as a community, though the centre of the village really only dates back to the 1860s.

CROWTHORNE

1925 / 78035

This part of east Berkshire consists almost entirely of
19th-century development; here and there are a few large
Victorian houses with huge plate-glass windows and free
Renaissance decorations.

LITTLE SANDHURST

1939 / 88875

Thirteen years before this photograph of Sandhurst was taken, the village police station was completed in memory of some of Sandhurst's older residents. The building was later converted into flats, with the bars removed from the cell windows.

SANDHURST

THE VILLAGE 1906 / 56999

The demand for peacetime army training led to the building of the Royal Military College early in the 19th century. This photograph of the Academy was taken about one hundred years after it moved here.

SANDHURST

THE ROYAL MILITARY COLLEGE 1911 / 64049

SANDHURST

1939 / 88867

Sandhurst has expanded enormously in the second half of the 20th century.
When this photograph was taken, at the outbreak of the Second World War, it
was a sleepy place in the shadow of the Royal Military College.

Wokingham's triangular market place is the town's focal point; it is dominated by its red brick Victorian town hall, which is triangular in shape and replaces a 17th-century timber-framed building.

WOKINGHAM

MARKET SQUARE 1906 / 57025A

During the Edwardian era, when this view was taken, Caversham was a popular address for affluent Reading residents. Much of the village lies on the north bank of the Thames, in the vicinity of the Henley road.

Caversham Bridge is one of Reading's most famous landmarks. The bridge played a key role in the Civil War: Charles I and Prince Rupert engaged in a fierce fight here against the Earl of Essex.

CAVERSHAM

THE BRIDGE 1904 / 52027

St Peter's Hill climbs out of the village towards Caversham's striking parish church of St Peter, which occupies a pleasant setting above the Thames. The tower can be seen from the river, peeping through the trees.

CAVERSHAM

ST PETER'S HILL   1908 / 59971

This photograph shows Bridge Street in the centre of Caversham, at the point where it crosses the Thames. The village became part of Berkshire in 1911, having previously been in neighbouring Oxfordshire.

CAVERSHAM

BRIDGE STREET 1908 / 59962

CAVERSHAM

FROM CAVERSHAM HEIGHTS 1908 / 59960

Caversham Heights lies to the north of the Thames and began to expand up the valley slopes when Caversham became a fashionable suburb of Reading.

Following the nationalisation of the railways in 1948, the Kennet and Avon Canal was closed to navigation in 1951, about four years before this photograph was taken.

THEALE

THE KENNET AND AVON CANAL C1955 / T254008

TILEHURST

SCHOOL ROAD   C1960 / T48027

Bustling School Road has long been lined with shops and houses. There used to be an old forge here, with a shed used for destroying unwanted horses and ponies.

READING

QUEEN VICTORIA STREET 1910 / 62201

Reading is one of those towns that can only be appreciated on foot. A walking tour of its main streets and thoroughfares reveals much of architectural interest - particularly in the vicinity of Queen Victoria Street.

Berkshire County Council's first Shire Hall, opened in 1911, a year before this photograph was taken. Adjacent to it are the stables (later the garage) of Suttons Seeds, once one of Reading's major employers, founded in 1806.

READING

SUTTONS SEEDS 1912 / 64639

READING

CAVERSHAM LOCK 1912 / 64648

Until 1911, a year before this photograph was taken, Caversham had always been in Oxfordshire. The merging of the village into the borough of Reading was strongly resisted by the residents of Caversham.

READING

BROAD STREET 1923 / 74436

During the early 1920s, Broad Street was a busy part of Reading, bustling with cars, trams and shoppers. There were many shops, including drapers, hat shops, gents' outfitters, shoe shops and a number of small cafes.

Two years before this photograph was taken, Reading Corporation was persuaded that Prospect Park should be bought 'for the benefit of weary workers who, when at rest, need some open space where communion with nature may be established'.

READING

PROSPECT PARK 1904 / 52022

St Mary's Butts is in the centre of Reading. The chequerboard flint and limestone tower of the church of St Mary's is a distinctive local landmark. The church dates back to Saxon times.

This photograph shows Kings Road at the point where it meets
Cemetery Junction, to the east of the town. Reading's population
expanded enormously during the 19th century, and many new homes
were built here.

READING,

KINGS ROAD 1924 / 76243

Buildings from several different periods overlook Reading's Market Place. At the centre of this picture is a distinctive stone lamp standard given by Edward Simeon in 1804 'as a mark of affection to his native town'.

READING

MARKET PLACE   1870 / R13001

Some of the original buildings in Hungerford High Street were destroyed by several fires. Wide streets are typical of country towns, designed so that markets could be held without blocking the main thoroughfare.

HUNGERFORD

Two hundred and thirty-five years before this photograph was taken, Samuel Pepys visited the town and ate 'very good troutes, eels and crayfish' at the Bear Hotel. Twenty years later, in 1688, William of Orange accepted the throne of England here.

HUNGERFORD

HIGH STREET 1903 / 49384

This view shows Bridge Street on the north bank of the Kennet and Avon canal. The canal and the railway brought prosperity to Hungerford, though the town's golden era began with the turnpiking of the Bath Road in the 18th century.

HUNGERFORD

BRIDGE STREET 1903 / 49386

*To the north of Newbury, on the edge of the downs, lies Hampstead
Norris, surrounded by hills and woodland. The church has an impressive
flint tower, Norman doorways and a splendid Jacobean roof to the nave.
The River Pang cuts through the village, as does the line of the former
Didcot to Southampton railway, which closed in 1964. Cattle are on
the move through the village. During the Second World War, Folly
Hill, which lies just outside the village, was the site of an airfield, with
Wellington bombers based here.*

HAMPSTEAD NORRIS

CHURCH STREET 1950 / H149011

NEWBURY

VICTORIA PARK C1955 / N61047

Victoria Park lies to the east of Newbury town centre. Covering an area of seventeen acres, the park includes a statue of Queen Victoria, guarded by two terracotta lions which originally stood in the Market Place.

NEWBURY

THE TOWN HALL   C1965 / N61076

On the right in this general view of Northbrook Street, photographed from beyond Timothy Whites & Taylors, is the imposing facade of Camp Hopson's department store, with its rubbed brickwork, Doric and Ionic pilasters, and tile-hung gables.

NEWBURY

NORTHBROOK STREET C1955 / N61062

One of Newbury's loveliest streets, Northbrook Street is famous for its mid to late Georgian buildings, and distinctive pink and blue brick houses above lines of modern shop fronts.

NEWBURY

NORTHBROOK STREET C1960 / N61078

This view of Northbrook Street shows the facade of Newbury's famous department store, Camp Hopson, established in 1921. This part of the building is mid-Georgian with a moulded cornice and pediment.

NEWBURY

NORTHBROOK STREET C1965 / N61111

Bartholomew Street, on the southern side of the town centre, was originally called West Street. This general view shows the street much as it is today - distinguished by its striking Georgian buildings.

NEWBURY

BARTHOLOMEW STREET
C1965   N61116

At the height of the canal era, the Wharf was a bustling depot where up to ten large barges could load and unload. The long, galleried Granary possibly dates back to the reign of Charles II, and is now part of the Museum.

NEWBURY

THE WHARF   C1960 / N61105

This general view of Northbrook Street shows the gable end to the left of the shop front, above which is a clock, which is all that remains of cloth-maker John Smallwood's house.

NEWBURY

NORTHBROOK STREET   C1965 / N61130

Situated between the River Thames and Quarry Woods, made famous in Kenneth Grahame's 'The Wind in the Willows', Bisham is one of Berkshire's most historic villages. The Abbey was originally a preceptory of the Knights Templar, and is mentioned in the Domesday Book. Queen Victoria is said to have called here whilst out driving in her carriage, but found no-one at home. This photograph captures some gentle activity on the Thames, with the tree-shrouded Abbey and church providing a splendid backdrop.

BISHAM

THE ABBEY AND THE CHURCH 1890 / 27237

A uniformed policeman is on duty in Maidenhead High Street. Among the town's more famous shops was Biggs, a high-class jeweller, where Queen Mary frequently purchased gifts when staying at nearby Windsor Castle.

MAIDENHEAD

HIGH STREET 1911 / 63797

At the height of the coaching era, Maidenhead was littered with posting inns either side of the High Street. Some of these hotels continued to thrive during the age of the motor car.

MAIDENHEAD

HIGH STREET   1921 / 70909

With its close proximity to London and its attractive riverside setting, Maidenhead became a fashionable resort in Victorian and Edwardian times, and was especially popular with wealthy Londoners, playboys and debutantes.

MAIDENHEAD

KING STREET 1904 / 52372

Typically, much of the older part of Maidenhead has long since disappeared, replaced by modern urban development. The original Town Hall in the High Street was a solid, sturdy building squeezed between lines of shops.

MAIDENHEAD

HIGH STREET AND TOWN HALL 1903 / 50833

This photograph shows the graceful architecture of Maidenhead Bridge, distinguished by its elegant arches, striking stonework and fine balustrade. The original bridge was built in the 13th century.

MAIDENHEAD

THE BRIDGE 1906 / 54099

Boulters Lock is one of the most famous landmarks on the River Thames, and during the Victorian and Edwardian periods drew large crowds of visitors in search of peaceful recreation. A boulter was another name for a miller.

MAIDENHEAD

BOULTERS LOCK 1925 /
77624

MAIDENHEAD

BOULTERS LOCK 1913 / 65542

Boulters Lock is probably the most famous lock on the Thames, and was the first and the lowest on the river of the first set of eight to be built under the legislation of 1770.

MAIDENHEAD

BOULTERS LOCK 1913 / 65543

MAIDENHEAD

BOULTERS LOCK 1906 / 54083

This photograph captures the Edwardian gaiety of the Thames at Boulters Lock, a particularly fashionable spot; here dozens of smart cruisers, punts and small craft parade before an admiring audience.

Many of Slough's town centre buildings are relatively new, dating from the post- and pre-war periods. However, parts of the town are Victorian, which gives an extra dimension to Slough's character.

SLOUGH

HIGH STREET 1961 / S256031

SLOUGH

HIGH STREET 1950 / S256003

Slough dates back to the 12th century, when it was a hamlet on the London to Bath road. The settlement later spread to the neighbouring parish of Stoke Poges.

The controversial artist Stanley Spencer was born in Cookham in 1891, seventeen years before this photograph was taken. The former Methodist chapel is now a gallery devoted to his work. Spencer used Cookham as the background to many of his paintings.

COOKHAM

HIGH STREET 1908 / 61017

This photograph shows the 17th-century Kings Arms Hotel, originally the Kings Head. A local woman once had her own special coinage for use only in the village, and a framed specimen of a half token still survives today.

COOKHAM

HIGH STREET 1914 / 67016

The Thames at Cookham used to have specifically-designed woven baskets for catching eels, which were set up at various points along the river. This view of the Thames illustrates Cookham's potential for picnicking and relaxing by the water's edge.

COOKHAM

ODNEY COMMON 1925 / 77588

In the early years of this century the village included an apothecary, a butcher's shop with traditional glazed tiles, a forge, dairy, a shoe-maker and an undertaker's. Everything the residents needed could be acquired locally.

COOKHAM

1914 / 67009

Transport has always played a key role in the history of Pangbourne. Its station on the Great Western Railway helped to widen its appeal as a popular inland resort. The ancient Ridgeway passes close to Pangbourne.

PANGBOURNE

THE VILLAGE 1910 / 62218

This photograph shows W H
Smith & Son on the left of the
picture, a few yards from the
road bridge crossing the River
Pang in the centre of the village.
W H Smith still occupies the
same premises today.

PANGBOURNE

THE VILLAGE 1910 / 62217

PANGBOURNE

THE VILLAGE 1910 / 62220

On the left is the facade of the 16th-century Cross Keys pub, one of Pangbourne's oldest buildings. Near it is Church Cottage, where Kenneth Grahame lived in the 1920s.

PANGBOURNE

THE BRIDGE AND THE GEORGE HOTEL   1899 / 42998

A late 19th-century advertisement for the George Hotel reads: 'This house, being in the centre of the picturesque scenery of Pangbourne, affords every accommodation for tourists, boating parties or anglers visiting the neighbourhood'.

PANGBOURNE

THE PANG 1890 / 27072

Whitchurch is Pangbourne's nearest neighbour. This photograph captures the atmosphere and feel of the village around the turn of the century. Sir John Soane, who rebuilt the Bank of England, was born here.

WHITCHURCH

THE ROYAL OAK 1899 / 43002

SONNING

1917 / 67959

Sonning was once the home of Dick Turpin's aunt. The Thames is crossed by an ancient 200-year-old bridge; the lock here regularly wins competitions for its *dazzling flower garden*.

Sonning includes many Georgian houses and timber-framed cottages.
Dick Turpin supposedly galloped through the village on his horse, Black
Bess, en route to his aunt's cottage after a hold-up on the Bath Road.

SONNING

THE VILLAGE 1904 / 52040

This view of Streatley shows the village centre. The Bull was once a coaching inn for the Royal Mail coach to Oxford. Early this century, much of Streatley was owned by the famous Morrell brewing family.

Many years before Wargrave grew in popularity as a riverside village, Edith, wife of Edward the Confessor, held the manor, and at that time it was known as 'Weregrave'.

WARGRAVE

THE VILLAGE 1890 / 27177

The village of Wargrave has an Edwardian feel to it, but its origins date back many centuries. The Bull, seen on the left, was once a popular coaching inn, close to the busy Bath Road.

WARGRAVE

HIGH STREET 1950 / W25002

Four years after this photograph was taken, the Thames burst its banks and floodwater raged through Bray. According to local sources, a fish was even caught in the high street.

BRAY

THE LANDING PLACE 1890 / 23621

BRAY

THE VILLAGE 1911 / 63821

This photograph of Bray shows the village centre, with the perpendicular chalk and stone tower of the parish church of St Michael peeping above the rooftops. The church dates from the time of Edward I and is built on the site of the original Norman church.

INDEX

PLEASE HELP US BRING FRITH'S PHOTOGRAPHS TO LIFE

Our authors do their best to recount the history of the places they write about. They give insights into how particular towns and villages developed, they describe the architecture of streets and buildings, and they discuss the lives of famous people who lived there. But however knowledgeable our authors are, the story they tell is necessarily incomplete.

Frith's photographs are so much more than plain historical documents. They are living proofs of the flow of human life down the generations. They show real people at real moments in history; and each of those people is the son or daughter of someone, the brother or sister, aunt or uncle, grandfather or grandmother of someone else. All of them lived, worked and played in the streets depicted in Frith's photographs.

We would be grateful if you would tell us about the many places shown in our photographs—the streets with their buildings, shops, businesses and industries. Describe your own memories of life in those streets: what it was like growing up there, who ran the local shop and what shopping was like years ago; if your workplace is shown tell us about your working day and what the building is used for now. With your help more and more Frith photographs can be brought to life, and vital memories preserved for posterity.

We will gradually add your comments and stories to the archive for the benefit of historians of the future. Wherever possible, we will try to include some of your comments in future editions of our books. Moreover, if you spot errors in dates, titles or other facts, please let us know, because our archive records are not always completely accurate—they rely on 150 years of human endeavour and hand-compiled records.

So please write, fax or email us with your stories and memories. Thank you!

FREE PRINT OF YOUR CHOICE

Choose any Frith photograph in this book.
Simply complete the Voucher opposite and
return it with your remittance for £2.25 (to
cover postage and handling) and we will print
the photograph of your choice in SEPIA (size
11 x 8 inches) and supply it in a cream mount
with a burgundy rule line
(overall size 14 x 11 inches).
**Please note: photographs with a reference number
starting with a "Z" are not Frith photographs and
cannot be supplied under this offer.**
Offer valid for delivery to UK one address only.

Mounted Print
Overall size 14 x 11 inches (355 x 280mm)

PLUS: **Order additional Mounted Prints at
HALF PRICE - £7.49 each** (normally £14.99)
If you would like to order more Frith prints
from this book, possibly as gifts for friends and
family, you can buy them at half price (with no
additional postage and handling costs).

PLUS: **Have your Mounted Prints framed**
For an extra £14.95 per print you can have your
mounted print(s) framed in an elegant polished
wood and gilt moulding, overall size
16 x 13 inches (no additional postage and
handling required).

IMPORTANT!

These special prices are only
available if you use this form to
order. You must use the ORIGINAL
VOUCHER (no copies permitted).

We can only despatch to one
UK address. This offer cannot be
combined with any other offer.

FRITH PRODUCTS AND SERVICES

All Frith photographs are available for you to buy as framed or mounted prints.
From time to time, other illustrated items such as Address Books and Maps are also
available. Already, almost 80,000 Frith archive photographs can be viewed and
purchased on the internet through the Frith website.

For more detailed information on Frith companies and products, visit:

www.francisfrith.co.uk

For further information, or trade enquiries, contact:

The Francis Frith Collection, Frith's Barn, Teffont, Salisbury SP3 5QP

Tel: +44 (0) 1722 716 376 Fax: +44 (0) 1722 716 881 Email: sales@francisfrith.co.uk

Voucher

for FREE
and Reduced Price
Frith Prints

Do not photocopy this voucher. Only the original is valid, so please fill it in, cut it out and return it to us with your order.

	Picture ref no	Page number	Qty	Mounted @ £7.49	Framed + £14.95	Orders Total £
1			1	Free of charge* £		£
2				£7.49	£	£
3				£7.49	£	£
4				£7.49	£	£
5				£7.49	£	£
6				£7.49	£	£

Please allow 28 days for delivery. Offer available to one UK address only

* Post & handling	£2.25
Total Order Cost	£

Title of this book . . . .

I enclose a cheque / postal order for £ . . . .
payable to 'The Francis Frith Collection'

OR debit my Mastercard / Visa / Maestro / Amex card

Card Number

Issue No (Maestro only)   Valid from (Amex/Maestro)

Expires   Signature

Name Mr/Mrs/Ms . . . .
Address . . . .
. . . .
. . . .
. . . . .Postcode. . . . .
Daytime Tel No . . . .
E-mail . . . .

Valid to 31/12/07